To Millie, God Blessing

Traveling With Bill

By Robert Joe (Bob) Williams

*Sincerely,
Bob Williams*

Copyright © 2015 Robert Joe Williams

All rights reserved.

ISBN:1523414863
ISBN-13:9781523414864

DEDICATION

With sincerity and lots of love I dedicate this book to my beautiful blended family, and to my primary family of Tulsa, Oklahoma. My three sisters (all deceased) always saw more in me than I saw in myself, especially my sister Eugenia, a gifted educator.

CONTENTS

	Acknowledgments	I
1	A December Day in Chicago	1
2	The Bus Trip	6
3	A Taste of Warmth	13
4	A Night to Remember	23
5	A New Day Arrives	26
	About the Author	29

ACKNOWLEDGMENTS

Thanks to the encouragement of Mr. and Mrs. Lewis Armstrong, this story became a printed reality. Their sincerity and spiritual friendship has been a blessing.

Special thanks to my wife Ruby, and daughter Artara E. Daniels for their involvement in encouraging, editing, and typing this story.

CHAPTER 1

A COLD DECEMBER DAY IN CHICAGO

Robert Joe Williams

1

2

Intimidating freezing cold weather had begun to cripple mobility in Chicago. It was December 1945 and Chicagoans were joyfully welcoming the surrender of Japan and the end of World War 11. Christmas was a few weeks away, a renewed sense of hopefulness and tranquility permeated the frigid air as Chicagoans attempted to redirect their lives and thoughts from four long years of wartime psychological weariness to a welcome post-war peace attitude.

Heavy snow silently blanketed the icy pavement as Bill trudged his way toward the downtown Greyhound Bus Terminal. Just another bitterly cold day in Chicago or the 'Windy

City' as it was frequently referred to when temperatures dipped uncomfortably below zero and outdoor activities are reduced to a minimum. Thinking of having to go to your place of employment, visit a neighbor or any outside activity became a lingering mental challenge. Cars and trucks rattled along with chains on tires. The coughing exhaust fumes collided with the freezing air transforming into streams of blue smoke. Overhead, elevated trains were clutching tracks and composing melodic tones heard only in winter's severest weather.

The cold curtailed some mechanical transportation and pedestrians, but not Bill, who year-round was conditioned to working outside in the inclement weather. For several months he had been anxiously awaiting the final week of the year - the time when he joyfully took a vacation from his prideful job as a construction laborer. Now, his thoughts were not on the bitter cold weather but on going home for Christmas to be with family and friends he had missed so deeply.

Although he moved slowly, Bill had equipped his body with several layers of garments for protection against the chilling wind. Even so, his face was exposed and the freezing temperature seemed to bite his watery eyes and wet nose.

Condensed moisture from his breath combined with falling snow to form a white mass of tiny ice crystals on his mustache and chin.

CHAPTER 2

THE BUS TRIP

He arrived at the bus terminal and found it fussily alive with holiday spirited people of varying economic levels. Many were holding assorted colors of cardboard boxes. Several had crying babies in tow, and noisy children grabbing food from grease-spotted shoe boxes. High spirited soldiers and sailors eagerly enroute to be a part of home encirclements and holiday gaiety.

Bill's towering, two hundred fifty pound frame forced him to stand out conspicuously in this melting maze of travelers as he meandered toward the ticket counter. A leathery, bronze complexion gave his perfect white teeth a highly visible background. A large, broad nose spread across his face, producing the appearance that his eyes were much too far apart. Each bear-like hand clutched and overused suitcase, displaying further physical evidence of an imposing personality. Had Bill been a younger man, one might easily have mistaken him for a professional football lineman.

His bulky presence always demanded respect. With his statue in this crowded terminal, emergency space seemed to develop wherever his giant feet took him.

"Roundtrip to Cleveland," Bill barked to the ticket clerk, obviously unable to conceal the pleasure in his voice. *"00* you mean Ohio?" she questioned.

"Yea, dat's where I'm going," he retorted, pushing forward a fist of crumpled dollar bills and giving the agent the heavier of the two suitcases-each of which was reinforced with rope tied around the outside.

Bill carefully stuffed the ticket into his inside jacket pocket, and then manipulated the right thumb and forefinger to button the coat. As a precautionary gesture, he gently patted the pocket where he had placed the ticket.

Standing around in the waiting room made Bill acutely aware of his aching feet, which pressed heavily

against over worn shoes. He
momentarily forgot about his
growing fatigue when a well-
dressed woman came near him to
gather her possessions to board
another bus. He briefly entertained
the thought of cuddling someone
so small and delicate.

Time drifted by as Bill
subconsciously observed the
continuous parade of diverse
people. He carefully lit a cigarette.
Slow streams of grayish-blue smoke
trickled from his wide nostrils,
adding to the haze throughout the
unattractive building.

Bill's ears perked to attention when
a distorted voice on the
loudspeaker system bellowed out

his bus and boarding gate number. A renewed surge of energy compelled him to quickly the join the rushing movement of pushing bodies. He detected scents of sweat and cheap perfume as he lifted himself up the steps of the bus.

Taking a cursory glance of the line of people behind him, it became evident to Bill that another bus was needed to accommodate all of these holiday travelers. Inwardly, he was just happy to have gotten on the first bus. He spotted an aisle seat near the rear and forced his remaining suitcase into the overhead luggage rack, and flopped his heavy body into the small seat.

A chorus of angry voices came

from passengers who were not allowed to board despite the drivers attempt to assure them that another bus had been called into service and would be arriving shortly. After the door was closed, there were several jerky movements as the driver backed the carrier from the curb, shifted into forward drive and headed toward the Dan Ryan Expressway, out of Chicago.

CHAPTER 3
A TASTE OF WARMTH

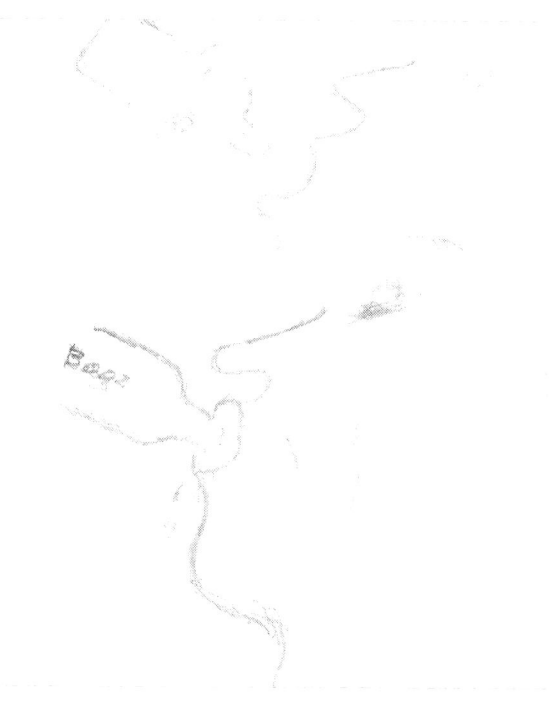

Bill's eyelids slowly grew too heavy to control and he soon surrendered to deep-echoed sleep. Later, a crying child disrupted his slumber and stopped his loud snoring. He wasn't sure how long he had slept, but he felt less fatigued now. As he attempted to check the time on his wristwatch, both eyes were distracted by the doleful landscape outside. A mass of snow was falling on the front window of the bus faster than the windshield wipers could remove it. Traffic on the freeway was greatly reduced, almost to a standstill.

"Your attention. Please," the bus driver demanded over the loudspeaker. "As a result of the growing accumulation of snow and very low visibility, we have been advised by headquarters to pull over as soon as we can locate an appropriate spot to do so, thank you for your patience" the driver concluded.

When some riders began uttering

concerns and gripes, the driver continued: "We are just being cautious, and we are sure this will blow over. We need your cooperation and understanding at this time.
Thank you."

Bill could feel the tension mounting. Guardedly, he took a small paper bag from his overcoat pocket, unscrewed the cap of the bottle concealed therein, and carefully lifted the container to his eagerly waiting taste buds. Bill softly smacked his large lips and cleared his throat in appreciation, while lowering the bottle and replacing the cap. Try as he may, it was hard to mask his facial felicity displayed after the drink.

An army sergeant standing in the aisle detected the liquor scent, looked at Bill's maneuvers and asked, "Say, Mate, would you happen to have any more of that?"

"Well, I recon I do," was Bill's smiling reply. Slowly rising from his seat, he took the old suitcase from the overhead luggage rack and opened it. Then, discretely, he passed a newspaper-wrapped object to the soldier.

The taunt sergeant unscrewed the bottle cap and, in a coordinated movement, his lips longingly embraced the mouth of the pint. He tilted his head backward for a prolong drink. Afterwards, in his excited stimulation, he attracted the attention of others nearby when he exclaimed, "Uhm! Uhm! That's some sho nuff good hooch."

Reaching into his hip pocket for his wallet, the soldier made a vague attempt to conceal his extended fist containing paper money for Bill.

"Is that enough? If it ain't, I'll give you some more," he said.

"Dis is fine," Bill replied, gladly accepting the five dollars, and very pleased by the sergeant's response to the homemade liquor.

Passengers soon found themselves leaning with the movement of the bus as the continuing heavy snow forced the driver to slowly negotiate the downward curve, pull off the freeway, and bring the bus to a gradual stop out of the path of other traffic.

Observers now tried to peer out the steamed-up windows to get a glimpse of their location.

They noticed that the bus was under a highway overpass, shielded from the snow. Sighs of relief echoed from their lips.

"Please try to make yourselves comfortable. I hope that we will not be here too long," the tired driver exclaimed.

Minutes later, the second bus pulled up behind. Hours passed and both carriers became immobile in the waist-deep accumulation of the soft, white crystalline flakes.

While snowbound, several persons seated near Bill and his newly found soldier friends were unable to conceal their appetites for the odoriferous liquid spirits.

A veteran sailor boldly left his seat near the front of the bus, walked to the rear and knelt by Bill. He inquired, "Is there anymore of that stuff?"

"Yea, I think I Kin come up wid some mo," was Bill's slow reply. He again went to the suitcase and exchanged the bottle for the green currency handed him. One by one, other passengers followed - all wanting whiskey to warm their chilled bodies.

Drivers of both buses recognized, with acceptance, their unanticipated dilemma and conferred briefly on several occasions. Each decided to put on a confident face while interacting with passengers.

The Cleveland bound bus driver didn't say so, but inwardly, he was especially grateful to Bill for helping him make the best of a bad situation. Going from seat to seat, he encouraged riders to relax and to be patient, and to go outside to a wooded area nearby whenever they needed to relieve themselves.

Arriving at Bill's seat, the driver leaned over and whispered something in his ear. "There is mo outside," Bill expressed to him, referring to additional bottles of liquor in his other suitcase locked in the luggage compartment.

"No problem. Let's go," the driver answered, dangling a chain of keys.

A group of men and women joyfully followed the pair outside and they all expressed excitement as they joined in removing bags and boxes from, the crowded storage area.

Upon seeing his aged bag "There, there it tis" Bill shouted, then gently picked up his battered suitcase.

A lengthy waiting line of persons formed behind the two bus drivers each eager and excited to purchase the homemade liquor.

CHAPTER 4

A NIGHT TO REMEMBER

Later, the falling snow began to gradually subside, turning into light occasional flakes before it completely stopped. Winter's darkness moved in and a small group of servicemen gathered logs from the wooded area nearby and built a fire close to the buses.

Soon a helicopter was sited circling overhead and dropped several bundles containing food, blankets and small radios.

"Don't worry, we'll get you out tomorrow morning," came an announcement from a loudspeaker on the low-flying aircraft.

With ample supplies and word of impending rescue, the travelers huddled around the bright burning fire where a mood of togetherness and mutual concern for one another lasted into the night. Soon, everyone was asleep.

First light of day mirrored a slow awakening of sunlight and new wintery warmth was welcomed. In an effort to maintain a small amount of heat in the buses, the large engines purred in idleness during the overnight stay.

Snow bound bus tires gradually pushed their way through the wet melting snow as they moved from the overnight under bridge shelter toward the approaching snow cleared highway.

CHAPTER 5

A NEW DAY ARRIVES

As the slow movement of the buses gently awakened bodies, sleep heavy eyes introduced a chorus of wakening yawns sounding a musical new day.

Heavy indulgent participants who had delighted in Bill's homemade alcoholic spirits began to give verbal delight in reliving the joy and comradery of the overnight fellowship. Bill was visibly overjoyed and financially rewarded that he was congratulated and embraced by all for making the overnight emergency stay a wonderful night to remember.

Both buses continued to their Cleveland destination with collective joyful inspired voices

Robert Joe Williams

giving musical sound to holiday
songs and sincere laughter.

ABOUT THE AUTHOR

Robert Joe (Bob) Williams a World War 11 veteran and native of Tulsa Oklahoma currently resides in Fayetteville, Georgia with his wife Ruby. Both are retired educators and are enjoying their second marriage of thirty-two years.

Bob authored "Traveling with Bill", a true story that was shared by an acquaintance in Cleveland Ohio.

Bob is proud to claim a blended family of seven adult children, ten grand children and six great grand children.

This is Bob's first published work.

Made in the USA
San Bernardino, CA
17 February 2016